"Advent creates people, new people."

Dietrich Bonhoeffer

Royalties from this book will be donated to
United Methodist Committee on Relief

Advent in Four Words

HOPE, PEACE, JOY, and LOVE

An Advent study by four
United Methodist bishops

Kenneth L. Carder
Sharma D. Lewis Logan
Robert D. Farr
Debra Wallace-Padgett

Market Square

Advent in Four Words

An Advent study by four United Methodist bishops

books@marketsquarebooks.com
141 N. Martinwood, Suite 2 Knoxville, Tennessee 37923

ISBN: 978-1-950899-93-7

Printed and Bound in the United States of America

Editor: Sheri Carder Hood
Cover Design: Kevin Slimp
Page Design: Carrie Rood
Post-Process Editor: Ashley Burton

Contents

INTRODUCTION

A Journey in Four Words

Advent is a season of tension and wonder, of deep longing and bright anticipation. It is the Church's invitation to pause before celebration, to wait with expectation rather than rush toward resolution. In an age of immediacy, Advent asks us to slow down. In a world crowded with noise and distraction, Advent beckons us into silence, reflection, and hope. It is no small thing to be asked to wait in a world like ours. And yet, each year, the Christian calendar opens not with a trumpet or a feast but with a breath: a beginning born in shadows when the promise of light feels like a fragile whisper.

Advent in Four Words invites us to listen closely to that whisper. Through the combined voices of four United Methodist bishops—Kenneth L. Carder, Robert D. Farr, Sharma D. Lewis Logan, and Debra Wallace-Padgett—we journey through the four weeks of Advent guided by four timeless and foundational words: *hope, peace, joy,* and *love.* These are not just themes for liturgical banners or candle-lighting services. They are theological anchors, scriptural declarations, and lived experiences. They name both our deepest needs and God's most enduring promises.

Each bishop brings a unique voice and pastoral insight to this devotional journey. Their reflections are shaped by years of ministry, seasons of loss and restoration, and a shared calling to guide the church through moments of trial and transformation. Together, their voices offer a harmonious and grounded perspective on how we might live more deeply into the story of God's coming, even amid the chaos of the season.

Using *Advent in Four Words* as a guide, the writers invite individuals, families, and congregations to travel through the season with intentionality and grace. Each daily reading includes a passage of scripture, a pastoral reflection, a heartfelt prayer, and a question for contemplation or group discussion. At the end of each week, a study guide offers further tools for reflection, conversation, and community engagement.

Living Between Two Promises

In Week One, Bishop Kenneth L. Carder opens the season with the profound reminder that Advent begins not with answers but with hope—hope grounded in the tension between two promises: the Messiah who has already come and the reign of God still on its way. Drawing from Matthew's Gospel and the apocalyptic imagery often overlooked during Christmas preparations, Bishop Carder explores what it means to wait faithfully in a world that often feels more like Good Friday than Christmas morning. Through images of daybreak and stories of personal loss and healing, he reminds us that the light of Christ dawns even in the darkest places. Hope, he writes, is not passive—it is a decision to live toward God's promise, even when the night feels long.

The Wonder of Preparation

In Week Two, Bishop Robert D. Farr leads us through the wilderness with peace as our guide. Drawing inspiration from John the Baptist and the prophet Isaiah, Bishop Farr reclaims "wonder" as a spiritual discipline. He asks what it means to prepare the road for Christ—not with perfection or certainty, but with curiosity, courage, and grace. His reflections brim with honesty and pastoral warmth, inviting us to rediscover the joy of preparing not only our homes but also our hearts. His repeated refrain—"I wonder..."—calls us back to a childlike openness to mystery, to questions that don't always have tidy answers. In a season where noise and division can overwhelm us, Bishop Farr urges us to shout not with anger but with "exuberant witness," preparing the way of peace in a weary world.

Joy that Sings through Sorrow

Week Three brings us into the presence of joy, not as a mere emotion, but as resilient faith. Bishop Sharma D. Lewis Logan offers reflections that are both personal and deeply pastoral, as well as theological. She writes with the voice of someone who has known grief and still proclaims joy. From the childhood rituals of church in Georgia to the painful memory of her mother's passing during Advent, Bishop Lewis Logan explores the paradox of joy in a season that often brings both light and loss. Her meditations remind us that joy is not the absence of sorrow but the presence of Christ in the midst of it. Through scripture, music, and memory, she invites us to trust that miracles still happen, that healing still comes, and that we are seen, known, and loved—even in our moments of sadness and struggle.

The Transforming Power of Love

In Week Four, Bishop Debra Wallace-Padgett guides us into the heart of love, the word that encompasses all others. Drawing from the nativity stories and the final days of Advent, she reflects on the vulnerability of God made flesh. Her devotions explore the quiet faith of Mary and Joseph, the generosity of the Magi, and the inclusivity of Christ's birth. She challenges us to recognize love not only as sentiment but as action—love that risks, love that forgives, love that seeks out the forgotten and the outsider. In a world where love is often transactional or conditional, Bishop Wallace-Padgett helps us see the radical, redeeming love of God that is freely given, calling us to respond with lives shaped by compassion, justice, and presence.

A Resource for Individuals and Communities

This devotional is structured to serve a wide range of readers. Whether you are reading quietly at dawn with a cup of coffee or gathering with a small group or

Sunday School class, *Advent in Four Words* is a tool for transformation. The daily readings provide a manageable rhythm for personal devotion, while the end-of-week group guides make it ideal for Sunday School classes, church-wide Advent studies, or neighborhood gatherings. Each section stands on its own but contributes to a larger journey, where scripture, reflection, and prayer converge to illuminate the path toward Christ.

What makes this book especially powerful is its blend of theological depth and pastoral accessibility. The bishops do not write from a distance; they speak as fellow pilgrims. They draw from the long tradition of the Church, as well as from the immediacy of their own experiences. This is not a book of abstract doctrines or spiritual clichés. It is a collection of honest meditations grounded in the Gospel and offered in the spirit of Advent's quiet urgency: *Prepare the way. The Lord is near.*

Come with Expectation

We live in a world that longs for renewal—a world fractured by injustice, loneliness, violence, and despair. And yet, into that very world, Christ is born again and again—not as an idea, but as a presence. As light. As love. This book will not solve every problem or answer every question. But it offers something more enduring: a way to walk through the season with awareness and intention, with scripture as our compass and these four words—hope, peace, joy, and love—as our lanterns.

Advent is a time of watching and waiting, of naming the brokenness while daring to believe in healing. It is a time of remembering the promise fulfilled in Bethlehem and leaning into the promise yet to come. This book is your companion on that journey. It invites you to bring your whole self—your doubts and your faith, your grief and your gratitude, your questions, and your quiet trust—and to walk once more toward the manger.

Come with expectation. Come with openness. Come with the hope, peace, joy, and love that are born anew in the light of Advent.

Kevin Slimp
Publisher, Market Square Books

First Week
of Advent

Bishop Kenneth L. Carder

First Sunday of Advent

Living between Two Promises

By Bishop Kenneth L. Carder

Scripture: Matthew 24:36-44

> *But about that day and hour no one knows, neither the angels of heaven, nor the Son, but only the Father. For as the days of Noah were, so will be the coming of the Son of Man. For as in the days before the flood they were eating and drinking, marrying and giving in marriage, until the day Noah entered the ark, and they knew nothing until the flood came and swept them all away, so, too, will be the coming of the Son of Man. Then two will be in the field; one will be taken, and one will be left. Two women will be grinding meal together; one will be taken and one will be left. Keep awake, therefore, for you do not know on what day your Lord is coming. But understand this: if the owner of the house had known in what part of the night the thief was coming, he would have stayed awake and would not have let his house be broken into. Therefore you also must be ready, for the Son of Man is coming at an hour you do not expect.*
>
> **Matthew 24:36-44 (NRSVue)**

Reflections

It's New Year's Day in the Christian year! The first Sunday in Advent marks a turning toward two promises. On the one hand, we are celebrating a promise already fulfilled in the birth of Jesus of Nazareth more than twenty centuries ago. We look back and remember stories about a virgin Mary giving birth to a son in a cattle stall, with visits from lowly shepherds and lofty wise men and the angels singing, "Peace on earth and good will toward people." The promise of the long-awaited-for Messiah has been fulfilled. "Joy to the world, the Lord has come!"

But that's only part of the story! Advent is far more than reveling in the memory of a distant promise fulfilled. Jesus' birth is a beginning, not an ending. He has come into the world as the One who embodies God's faithfulness in the past and God's promise of a new future. Advent, then, is a season of remembering and anticipating, celebrating what has been and anticipating what will be.

The early Christians lived with the tension between these two promises. The Gospel of Matthew was written amid that tension. On the one hand, the stories of Jesus' birth, his life and teachings, his death and resurrection circulated widely and were fresh in their minds. These stories had brought them together. Their lives were being shaped, guided, and inspired by the memories of Jesus. They sought to follow his way of living. They trusted the promise that his reign, what he called the "kingdom of heaven," would come to fulfillment, perhaps in their lifetime. He had promised that God's reign would come on earth as it is in heaven!

Yet, the world was dominated by the Roman Empire. The way of life described in Jesus' Sermon on the Mount and summarized by love for God and neighbor was a stark contrast to the prevailing cruelty, exploitation, oppression, and violence. Holding on to the promise of the conquest of love over hate, forgiveness over retribution, justice over exploitation, and peace over brute force was the challenge.

That's the reality behind what is called "the little apocalypse" in Matthew 24. The writer is urging the community to hang on to both God's faithfulness in the past and the consummation of God's promise of a new heaven and new earth. The current turbulent world of persecution, violence, destruction, and uncertainty is not the final word.

But how can we live with such tension? What are we to do in the meantime?

Watch! Stay alert! Keep awake! The signs are there, in unexpected places. You aren't alone! Stay together! Support one another!

Live now as though God's promise in Jesus the Christ has already been fulfilled! Love now! Forgive now! Show mercy now! Walk humbly now! Seek peace today! Serve generously now!

In so doing, the promise of Jesus' return will come closer to fulfillment—in us.

Prayer

We thank you, O God, for your fulfilled promise in the coming of Jesus. Enable us to live in accordance with his life, teachings, death, and resurrection as we expectantly wait for the final triumphant of your Reign. Amen.

Question

How does the memory of God's faithfulness and God's promise of a new future enable you to live with hope and courage amid today's challenges?

First Monday of Advent

Be Ready

By Bishop Kenneth L. Carder

Scripture: Matthew 24:42-44

> *Keep awake, therefore, for you do not know on what day your Lord is coming. But understand this: if the owner of the house had known in what part of the night the thief was coming, he would have stayed awake and would not have let his house be broken into. Therefore you also must be ready, for the Son of Man is coming at an hour you do not expect.*
>
> **Matthew 24:42-44 (NRSVue)**

Reflections

The notion of "end times," "rapture," and "second coming" spawned the popular *Left Behind* series written by Tim LaHaye and Jerry B. Jenkins. The books and spin-off movies rely heavily on images from apocalyptic writings, particularly the book of Revelation. More than sixty-five million copies have been sold in various languages. Although the books and movies distort and misuse the Bible's apocalyptic images, they capture the sense of urgency and crisis present in Matthew 24 and similar writings.

Those apocalyptic images dominated the sermons I heard as a child. I had terrifying nightmares of my parents being taken to heaven with me being left behind. Preachers vividly declared that the cataclysmic end of the world foretold in the Bible was about to take place. Signs of the End were clear! Judgment was on its way. We had better get ready, or else we would be among those suffering "the great tribulation" where there would be "weeping and wailing and gnashing of teeth."

The way to get ready was to come to the altar, repent of our sins, and accept Jesus as our Lord and Savior. Fear of being left behind, condemned to earthly tribulations and eternal damnation led many to the altar and public confession of faith in Jesus.

While the promise of the End and Second Coming includes crisis and judgment, the purpose of such promises is hope, not fear; expectancy, not dread; courage, not retreat.

Apocalyptic writings, exemplified by Matthew 24, emerge from periods of persecution, suffering, and oppression. The purpose is to assure the faithful that God's promised future will come to fulfillment. God's Reign in Jesus the Christ is sovereign over the systems of domination in this world. Hatred, cruelty, injustice, poverty, environmental degradation, violence, and war will not have the last word.

The Reign of God that we see in the birth, life, teachings, death, and resurrection of Jesus is the way of the future. As my friend Tex Sample often says, "God bats last, and it's a walk-off home run!"

The way to get ready for the End is to turn toward that world of God's present and final reign and to be a sign of Christ's Coming. We prepare for the future coming of the Son of Man by living each moment in accordance with Jesus' way of love, compassion, justice, and mercy. Each act of love amid the world's suffering and tribulation points toward the final victory of God's triumph over the powers and principalities of this world.

Prayer

Sovereign God, in the coming of Jesus the Christ, you have made known your final victory over all that threatens your reign of compassion, justice, generosity, and joy. Open our eyes to see signs of your reign in these turbulent times, and through the power of your Spirit, enable us to be a sign of your final reign. Amen.

Question

How might the images of the End as portrayed in apocalyptic writings give us hope and courage to live now in light of God's final triumph?

First Tuesday of Advent

Warning, Challenge, and Vision

By Bishop Kenneth L. Carder

Scripture: Isaiah 2:1-5

> *The word that Isaiah son of Amoz saw concerning Judah and Jerusalem.*
>
> *In days to come the mountain of the LORD's house shall be established as the highest of the mountains and shall be raised above the hills; all the nations shall stream to it. Many peoples shall come and say, "Come, let us go up to the mountain of the LORD, to the house of the God of Jacob, that he may teach us his ways and that we may walk in his paths." For out of Zion shall go forth instruction and the word of the LORD from Jerusalem.*
>
> *He shall judge between the nations and shall arbitrate for many peoples; they shall beat their swords into plowshares and their spears into pruning hooks; nation shall not lift up sword against nation, neither shall they learn war any more. O house of Jacob, come, let us walk in the light of the LORD!*
>
> **Isaiah 2:1-5 (NRSVue)**

Reflections

It was a time of grave crisis! National collapse loomed on the near horizon as Assyrian aggression advanced. Economic disparity prevailed, and the poor were either ignored or exploited. Crime and violence filled the streets. Suffering and death abounded as the prophet declared, "From head to toe, none are well—only bruises, cuts, and raw wounds, not treated, not bandaged, not soothed with oil" (Isaiah 1:6, NRSVue).

Political and religious leaders were oblivious to the plight of the people and complicit in the injustices and oppression. Faithfulness to God, who formed the nation to be a beacon of justice and righteousness, had drifted into idolatrous worship of culturally prevailing gods.

Amid the crisis, Isaiah issues a warning, a challenge, and a promise. The prophet warned that the prevailing injustice and idolatry created widespread suffering and initiated the approaching national collapse. He challenged the people to repent and follow the God who "defends the orphans, widows, and sojourners." And Isaiah promised that the future belongs to God's shalom, God's peace.

The season of Advent includes the three components of Isaiah's message! We are summoned to be alert to and name the injustices and idolatries that are creating suffering and death in our national life.

We are challenged to repent of our own participation in practices and policies that are contrary to God's revelation in scripture and supremely in Jesus.

And we are invited to contribute to the coming of God's shalom/peace by transforming instruments of violence into implements of compassion.

Prayer

God of compassion and justice, open our eyes to see the injustice and suffering around us. Grant us the humility necessary to acknowledge our own failures to live justly and compassionately, and grant us the courage to live now in the light of your reign brought near in Jesus Christ, who is the "Prince of Peace." Amen.

Question

What gives you hope amid the turmoil, suffering, and trauma in today's world?

First Wednesday of Advent

Meeting God in Particular Places

By Bishop Kenneth L. Carder

Scripture: Psalm 122:1-5

I was glad when they said to me, "Let us go to the house of the LORD!"

Our feet are standing within your gates, O Jerusalem

Jerusalem—built as a city that is bound firmly together.

To it the tribes go up, the tribes of the LORD, as was decreed for Israel, to give thanks to the name of the LORD.

For there the thrones for judgment were set up, the thrones of the house of David.

Psalm 122:1-5 (NRSVue)

Reflections

It was a seminary class discussion more than sixty years ago. The professor of Old Testament commented on the popular notion that one can worship God anywhere since God's presence is boundless.

Dr. Lowell Hazzard stated: "It's true, we can connect with God at any place and any time. But unless there is a particular place and time where we intentionally connect with God, it is highly unlikely that we will meet God anywhere."

Across the centuries, Jerusalem has been a "particular place" for meeting God by followers of the three Abrahamic faiths: Judaism, Christianity, and Islam. Its elevated location appropriately expresses the lofty role the city plays in religious experience and history. Traditionally, it is there in Jerusalem that God has been especially present. Even now, people of the faith make visits to the city's special sites, such as the "Wailing Wall," with a sense of reverence and awe.

But to the Jewish people returning to their homeland following the Babylonian exile in the sixth century BCE, the rebuilt city and temple took on added significance. Pilgrimages were made to the city to celebrate special festivals, including the Passover and the celebration of deliverance from Egyptian bondage.

Psalm 122 is a "pilgrimage song" sung by Jewish pilgrims as they approached Jerusalem, the Holy City—a place of sanctuary, safety, and refuge. The very dirt on which they walked, the architecture of its walls and buildings, and the stones that comprised the temple were viewed as signs of God's presence and mighty acts of salvation. Jerusalem was a visible reminder of Israel's past and future glory, an expansive symbol of God's reign of justice, righteousness, and peace/shalom.

We all need icons and places that remind us of God's steadfast love and faithfulness that point us toward a future of hope. The church exists as such a place. The space has been dedicated for worship, fellowship, formation, and service for the people of God. Through the liturgy, we remember and rehearse God's mighty acts of salvation, hear the divine word proclaimed, share in the sacraments, and support one another in living toward God's present and coming reign in Jesus Christ.

Prayer

God, whose presence knows no boundaries of space and time, enable us to meet you in particular places and at special times. May each encounter with you empower us to live hopefully toward your reign in Jesus the Christ. Amen.

Questions

Where are the specific places you experience the presence and power of God?

Can you identify an object, icon, or symbol that regularly points you toward the Holy and inspires you to live faithfully and hopefully?

First Thursday of Advent

The Things that Make for Peace

By Bishop Kenneth L. Carder

Scripture: Psalm 122:6-9

Pray for the peace of Jerusalem:
"May they prosper who love you.

Peace be within your walls,
and security within your towers."

For the sake of my relatives and friends
I will say, "Peace be within you."

For the sake of the house of the LORD our God
I will seek your good.

Psalm 122:6-9 (NRSVue)

Reflections

As a faithful member of the Jewish community, Jesus made many pilgrimages to Jerusalem. He likely sang Psalm 122 as he approached the Holy City. The concluding verses of the psalm are a prayer for the prosperity and peace of Jerusalem and its citizens and a commitment to seek the good of the city.

Matthew and Luke report one occasion when Jesus likely prayed this psalm as he approached Jerusalem. He was approaching the city to celebrate Passover. Opposition to him was reaching a crisis point. Now he would be entering the center of religious and political power with the events of what we call Holy Week looming before him.

As the vision of Jerusalem loomed in the distance, his prayer was a tearful lament: "Jerusalem, Jerusalem, the city that kills the prophets and stones those who are sent to it! How often have I desired to gather your children together as a hen gathers her brood under her wings, and you were unwilling" (Matthew 23:37, NRSVue)!

Luke closely connects Jesus' lament with the petition in Psalm 122 as he writes: "As he came near and saw the city, he wept over it, saying, "If you, even you, had only recognized on this day the things that make for peace" (Luke 19:41-42, NRSVue)!

While Jerusalem was the traditional place for meeting God and remembering God's mighty acts of salvation and deliverance, it was also a place of conflict, bloodshed, and exploitation. The city that was built and set apart to bear witness to God's shalom/peace would soon kill the One who was "the Prince of Peace."

It is a somber warning and poignant plea to us. The places and institutions set apart as sacred reminders and practitioners of God's presence and purposes can become centers of conflict, division, cruelty, and violence. How often have we as the church resisted and inflicted violence on those whom God has sent and failed to recognize "the things that make for peace."

What does it mean to pray for the peace of the city and to seek its good? Perhaps our most sincere prayer is one of lament and humble repentance. Individually and collectively, we fail to embody and follow the way of Jesus. He has shown us "the things that make for peace," and we have trusted and followed the things that contribute to hatred, division, and violence.

Still, the One who is the incarnation of God seeks to "gather us together as a hen gathers her brood under her wings."

Prayer

Gracious God, forgive our failure to live the way of Jesus and thereby contributing to the division and brokenness in the world. Help us to know and do the things that make for peace by welcoming and following the Prince of Peace, in whose name we pray. Amen.

Question

In what ways is your church contributing to peace?

First Friday of Advent

What Time Is It?

By Bishop Kenneth L. Carder

Scripture: Romans 13:8-14

Owe no one anything, except to love one another, for the one who loves another has fulfilled the law. The commandments, "You shall not commit adultery; you shall not murder; you shall not steal; you shall not covet," and any other commandment, are summed up in this word, "You shall love your neighbor as yourself." Love does no wrong to a neighbor; therefore, love is the fulfilling of the law.

Besides this, you know what time it is, how it is already the moment for you to wake from sleep. For salvation is nearer to us now than when we became believers; the night is far gone; the day is near. Let us then throw off the works of darkness and put on the armor of light; let us walk decently as in the day, not in reveling and drunkenness, not in illicit sex and licentiousness, not in quarreling and jealousy. Instead, put on the Lord Jesus Christ, and make no provision for the flesh, to gratify its desires.

Romans 13:8-14 (NRSVue)

Reflections

Studies indicate that the perception of time changes as we age. For children, it passes slowly. It seems that the anticipated events will never come—Christmas, birthdays, summer. When we are young, time appears to be abundant and inexhaustible.

As the years accumulate, time passes faster. The hours, days, months, and years seem to speed up. That's certainly my experience as I live into my eighties. I easily lose track of the hours, even days, as they quickly fade.

My smartwatch tells me what time it is and prods me with occasional reminders, such as "It's time to stand up," "It's time to prepare for bed," or "You have an appointment at 10 a.m."

Another change is the stark awareness that I'm running out of time. Death is claiming more family members, friends, and colleagues. Physical ailments become intimations of impending frailty. The end draws closer.

The Apostle Paul alerts us to the importance of knowing what time it is! But he's talking about far more than the time we mark by the calendar and clock. That's *chronos,* chronological time. Paul is thinking about another kind of time: *kairos,* God's time.

Paul is keenly aware that in Jesus Christ, time itself has been transformed. God's kairos has entered chronos, and a new age has dawned. The eternal has invaded the temporal and filled every moment with new possibilities, new meaning, and new expectancy.

What time is it? It's Advent: God has entered our time and space in Jesus of Nazareth and claimed all time—past, present, and future—as the realm of God's reign of love and justice.

Salvation is near! It's time to live in the present as though God's future is NOW! It's time to fill each moment with behaviors and values incarnate in Jesus. It's time to love one another as Christ loves us as an intimation of the time when God's reign in Jesus Christ will be complete.

Prayer

Loving God, in Jesus Christ, you have claimed all time and space as the realm of your saving presence and power. Help us live each moment with attentiveness to your presence and with faithfulness to your love as made known in Jesus, in whose name we pray. Amen.

Questions

How has your perception of time changed over the years?

What are the implications for how you live in the present?

First Saturday of Advent

Living at Daybreak

By Bishop Kenneth L. Carder

Scripture: Romans 13:11-14

> *Besides this, you know what time it is, how it is already the moment for you to wake from sleep. For salvation is nearer to us now than when we became believers; the night is far gone; the day is near. Let us then throw off the works of darkness and put on the armor of light; let us walk decently as in the day, not in reveling and drunkenness, not in illicit sex and licentiousness, not in quarreling and jealousy. Instead, put on the Lord Jesus Christ, and make no provision for the flesh, to gratify its desires.*
>
> **Romans 13:11-14 (NRSVue)**

Reflections

Daybreak is my favorite time of the day. I almost always wake up before sunrise. Walks at dawn have been among my most memorable, meaningful experiences. One such walk was especially profound, even transformative.

It was August 2020, ten months after the death of Linda, my wife of fifty-eight years. I was on a predawn walk at Lake Junaluska, where Linda and I had shared sixty years of memories. I was walking westward around the lake as the first glimmers of the new day arose in the east. Suddenly, the emerging rays from the sun began lighting the world. I turned eastward and watched as bursts of brilliant radiance peeked over the distant hills. The radiant beams of morning slowly dispelled the clouds and lingering shadows of night, revealing the surrounding beauty and promise of a new day.

Awe snapped my grieving soul to attention. As the rising sun dispelled the night's lasting shadows, the haunting grief from a lost yesterday was wrapped in a new garment of abiding love, pervasive beauty, and relentless hope. Though loss and grief remained, a new future awaited, filled with promise and meaning.

That experience at daybreak has become a metaphor for the meaning of Advent and today's scripture reading from Romans. For Paul, God in Jesus Christ brings into a being a New Creation. In Jesus' life, teaching, death, resurrection, and ascension, a new world has come into being. It is a world filled with the incarnate presence of the creating, liberating, reconciling, and transforming grace of God. Jesus' coming is like the sun rising at daybreak!

Yet, the vestiges of night remain! Darkness still casts its gloom. The dark deeds of self-preoccupation, sin, and death persist in their destructiveness. Indeed, the emerging light exposes those deeds more clearly, tempting us to shield ourselves from the light and remain in the darkness.

Paul declares the coming of Christ Jesus is like the sun rising at daybreak. A new day has dawned, filled with the incarnate presence of the creating, liberating, reconciling, transforming grace of God. He called it a New Creation, a new way of being in the world.

It's time to "throw off the works of darkness and put on the armor of light." The old, dark world of sin and death, hatred and division, despair and violence is coming to an end. Now is the time to take off the garments of nighttime, "put on the Lord Jesus Christ," and walk in the light of God's present and coming reign of compassion, justice, hospitality, generosity, and peace.

Advent is daybreak! The coming of Jesus marks the dawning of a new day. A new world has come into being, a world of Incarnate Love. Though the vestiges of nighttime remain, we live confidently toward that Day when dawn's early light shines in noonday brilliance over all creation, and Christ is all in all.

Prayer

God, who has inaugurated a new creation in the coming of Jesus the Christ and through Christ has conquered the powers of sin and death: through your grace and the power of the Holy Spirit, enable us to cast off the works of darkness, put on the garments of love as revealed in Jesus Christ, and live toward the new future with hope and love. Amen.

Question

What is your response to the daybreak metaphor for Advent and the coming of Christ?

GROUP STUDY GUIDE

First Week of Advent

Living Between Two Promises

In week One of Advent, drawing from scripture and personal experience, Bishop Carder calls the church to embody God's reign through love, justice, mercy, and vigilance in a world still marked by suffering and darkness. Advent, he writes, is like daybreak—a new creation dawning with the presence of Christ, calling us to walk in the light even as night's shadows linger.

Welcome and Opening Prayer (5 minutes)

Invite a group member to open with one of the provided daily prayers or a prayer of their own.

Scripture Reading (5-10 minutes)

Read aloud one or more of the week's key scriptures:

Matthew 24:36-44, 42-44

Isaiah 2:1-5

Psalm 122:1-5, 6-9

Romans 13:8-14

Discussion Questions (30–35 minutes)

Use the questions below to foster conversation. Encourage honest sharing and mutual support.

Living Between Two Promises (Matthew 24:36-44)

How do you personally balance remembering Christ's first coming and hoping for his return?

In what ways can your daily life reflect both remembrance and anticipation?

Hope in Apocalyptic Language (Matthew 24:42-44)

What feelings do you associate with the "end times"? Fear? Hope? Confusion?

How might re-framing apocalyptic texts as sources of hope reshape your faith journey?

The Prophetic Call to Justice (Isaiah 2:1-5)

What modern "swords" might we be called to turn into "plowshares" today?

Where do you see injustice, and how might your faith lead you to respond?

Sacred Places and Encountering God (Psalm 122:1-5)

Where have you personally felt closest to God?

How can we honor sacred spaces while remembering God meets us everywhere?

The Things that Make for Peace (Psalm 122:6-9)

How is your church or community seeking peace in practical ways?

What role might lament and repentance play in becoming peacemakers?

Time and Urgency in Advent (Romans 13:8-14)

How has your perception of time changed in different seasons of life?

What does it mean for you to "put on the armor of light" this Advent?

Closing Time (5 minutes)

Prayer: Choose one of the week's prayers or invite a group member to close in prayer.

Challenge: Encourage each person to take one action this week that reflects God's reign of love, justice, or hope.

Second Week

of Advent

Bishop Bob Farr

Second Sunday of Advent

I Wonder

By Bishop Bob Farr

Scripture: Matthew 3:1-12

While Jesus was living in the Galilean hills, John, called "the Baptizer," was preaching in the desert country of Judea. His message was simple and austere, like his desert surroundings: "Change your life. God's kingdom is here."

John and his message were authorized by Isaiah's prophecy:

Thunder in the desert!
Prepare for God's arrival!
Make the road smooth and straight!

John dressed in a camel-hair habit tied at the waist by a leather strap. He lived on a diet of locusts and wild field honey. People poured out of Jerusalem, Judea, and the Jordanian countryside to hear and see him in action. There at the Jordan River those who came to confess their sins were baptized into a changed life.

When John realized that a lot of Pharisees and Sadducees were showing up for a baptismal experience because it was becoming the popular thing to do, he exploded: "Brood of snakes! What do you think you're doing slithering down here to the river? Do you think a little water on your snakeskins is going to make any difference?

It's your life that must change, not your skin! And don't think you can pull rank by claiming Abraham as father. Being a descendant of Abraham is neither here nor there. Descendants of Abraham are a dime a dozen. What counts is your life. Is it green and flourishing? Because if it's deadwood, it goes on the fire.

"I'm baptizing you here in the river, turning your old life in for a kingdom life. The real action comes next: The main character in this drama—compared to him I'm a mere stagehand—will ignite the kingdom life within you, a fire within you, the Holy Spirit within you, changing you from the inside out. He's going to clean house—make a clean sweep of your lives. He'll place everything true in its proper place before God; everything false he'll put out with the trash to be burned."

Matthew 3:1-12 (MSG)

Reflections

John the Baptist is always an interesting character to read about and study—though I am not sure we would appreciate him very much in our present lives. He's a figure easier left to the pages of scripture than actualized in our modern-day faith journey. Nevertheless, there is John, right in the middle of Jesus' early life development.

John's preaching comes right out of the Prophet Isaiah's writings, "The voice of one shouting in the desert, 'prepare a road for the Lord, make straight a path for Him to travel.'"

I wonder, what roads do we need to prepare for Jesus today? I wonder, what shouting do we need to do to get ready? In our world today, a great deal of shouting is taking place, a lot of noise is being made, and many injustices are occurring.

I wonder, do we have the courage of John the Baptist? I wonder, do we have the willingness to prepare the necessary roads for the arrival of Christ into our lives and the world? I wonder, do we need a little more of John the Baptist's courage to speak out? On the other hand, I wonder if John showed more grace elsewhere in his ministry to complement the pushiness.

I wonder what all Jesus and John talked about in this encounter at the edge of the desert. I wonder what led Jesus to decide to get baptized a little later in the story. I wonder …

This year, in this Advent season, I've been wondering.

Wonder is a part of the Christmas season for children and adults alike. Wonder … I wonder, is wonder a precursor to the early stages of faith?

Advent starts with a baby born in an out-of-the-way place called Bethlehem to unwed, young, poor parents. I wonder what God was thinking.

I pray that you receive the gift of wonder this Advent. The Prophet Isaiah was so full of wonder that he wrote a poem about the coming of a Messiah. I'm not into poetry, but this one is worth reading.

A green Shoot will sprout from Jesse's stump,
from his roots a budding Branch.
The life-giving Spirit of God will hover over him,
the Spirit that brings wisdom and understanding,
The Spirit that gives direction and builds strength,
the Spirit that instills knowledge and Fear-of-God.
Fear-of-God
will be all his joy and delight.

He won't judge by appearances,
won't decide on the basis of hearsay.
He'll judge the needy by what is right,
render decisions on earth's poor with justice.
His words will bring everyone to awed attention.
A mere breath from his lips will topple the wicked.
Each morning he'll pull on sturdy work clothes and boots,
and build righteousness and faithfulness in the land.

A Living Knowledge of God

The wolf will romp with the lamb,
the leopard sleep with the kid.
Calf and lion will eat from the same trough,
and a little child will tend them.
Cow and bear will graze the same pasture,
their calves and cubs grow up together,
and the lion eat straw like the ox.
The nursing child will crawl over rattlesnake dens,
the toddler stick his hand down the hole of a serpent.
Neither animal nor human will hurt or kill
on my holy mountain.
The whole earth will be brimming with knowing God-Alive,
a living knowledge of God ocean-deep, ocean-wide.

Isaiah 11:1-10 (MSG)

I wonder ...

Can I see the star again?

Can I smell the animals in the stable?

Can I visualize the kings delivering their gifts?

Can I hear the angels sing?

Can I find the courage to shout out, "Messiah, Savior, King, Friend, Jesus?"

I wonder ...

The word wonder is used fifteen times in the scriptures, reminding us that something deeper and greater is at work, something beyond the obvious. I love the phrase in Acts 3 where the believers were "filled with awe and wonder." Maybe it's because the followers could see something deeper. Acts 3 says, "Many miracles and wonders occurred." Perhaps we need more awe and wonder in our own lives. Maybe we should look a little deeper. In the heart of the Christmas story lies a profound wonder that helps us see beyond the ordinary.

Luke 2:19 is one of my favorite lines in the Bible: "Mary remembers all these things and thought deeply about them." John the Baptist saw something deeper in his cousin Jesus, so much so that he dedicated his life to helping people prepare for Jesus, guiding them to see the new thing in Christ Jesus.

I wonder, can we see it—so that we, too, like old Simeon from Luke, might proclaim, "With my own eyes I have seen your salvation which you prepared for in the presence of all peoples" (Luke 2:30). A great light has been revealed: Jesus Christ. I wonder, can we see it?

Prayer

Lord, in this Advent season, stir in us the courage of John, the awe of Mary, and the wonder of a child, that we might see Your light and prepare the way for Your coming anew.

Questions

What does it mean for you to prepare the way for Christ today?

Where in your life might God be inviting you to rediscover the gift of wonder?

Second Monday of Advent

I Wonder, What Roads Do We Need to Prepare for Jesus Today?

By Bishop Bob Farr

Scripture: Matthew 3:1-3 and Isaiah 11:1-5

While Jesus was living in the Galilean hills, John, called "the Baptizer," was preaching in the desert country of Judea. His message was simple and austere, like his desert surroundings: "Change your life. God's kingdom is here."

John and his message were authorized by Isaiah's prophecy:

Thunder in the desert!
Prepare for God's arrival!
Make the road smooth and straight!

Matthew 3:1-3 (MSG)

A green Shoot will sprout from Jesse's stump,
from his roots a budding Branch.
The life-giving Spirit of God will hover over him,
the Spirit that brings wisdom and understanding,
The Spirit that gives direction and builds strength,
the Spirit that instills knowledge and Fear-of-God.
Fear-of-God
will be all his joy and delight.
He won't judge by appearances,
won't decide on the basis of hearsay.
He'll judge the needy by what is right,
render decisions on earth's poor with justice.

His words will bring everyone to awed attention.
A mere breath from his lips will topple the wicked.
Each morning he'll pull on sturdy work clothes and boots,
and build righteousness and faithfulness in the land.

Isaiah 11:1-5 (MSG)

Reflections

It seems there is always road construction in any direction when driving from my home or office to any destination in Missouri. The delays it causes can be frustrating, but I know that with each orange cone, progress is being made. At some point, when the construction is complete, the road will be smooth and easier to drive. However, it is difficult to be patient during the preparation and construction of the road.

John the Baptist declared the prophecy to prepare for God's arrival, to make the road smooth and straight. I enjoy driving my 1967 Falcon over straight, paved roads where traffic is sparse because I can fully experience the speed for which the engine was designed. When I drive on a straight road, it's easier and faster.

I wonder, what road do we need to be preparing for ourselves and others for Jesus' smooth and easy arrival this Advent? How do we build those roads with the people with whom we regularly interact? Like road construction, patience with the process is vital. Isaiah 11 tells us the Spirit brings wisdom and understanding, direction, and builds strength. In this season of preparing for the arrival of Christ, what if we allowed the Spirit to build and smooth out the roads to each other, "not judged by appearances and not decided on the basis of hearsay"? What if, instead, we allow the Holy Spirit to do the construction, creating "awed attention" in our hearts and inspiring us to interact with each other with patience, knowing the work will "build righteousness and faithfulness in the land."

Prayer

Lord, as we wait and prepare this Advent, smooth the roads of our hearts, build in us the patience to trust Your timing, and guide us by Your Spirit to create paths of peace, love, and righteousness for You and for one another. Amen.

Question

What roads do you need to prepare as we await the arrival of Jesus?

Second Tuesday of Advent

I Wonder, What Shouting Do We Need to Do?

By Bishop Bob Farr

Scripture: Psalm 72:1-7

Give the gift of wise rule to the king, O God,
the gift of just rule to the crown prince.
May he judge your people rightly,
be honorable to your meek and lowly.
Let the mountains give exuberant witness;
shape the hills with the contours of right living.
Please stand up for the poor,
help the children of the needy,
come down hard on the cruel tyrants.
Outlast the sun, outlive the moon—
age after age after age.
Be rainfall on cut grass,
earth-refreshing rain showers.
Let righteousness burst into blossom
and peace abound until the moon fades to nothing.

Psalm 72:1-7 (MSG)

Reflections

I wonder, what shouting do we need to do to be ready? In our world today, a great deal of shouting is taking place, a lot of noise is being made, and many injustices are occurring. I admit, I can do my share of shouting, which may not be my best characteristic. And I don't like being shouted at. Honestly, does anyone like to be shouted at? So, what does it mean to shout in a way that prepares us and others for the arrival of Jesus?

In Psalm 72, the psalmist says, "Let the mountains give exuberant witness." Exuberant is an interesting word. It means filled with or characterized by lively energy and excitement. Maybe it is really about what the shouting is characterized by and what is being shared.

Jumping ahead to the Christmas story, the Angels on High sang the message of Jesus' arrival to the shepherds. It could be said that they gave an exuberant witness, a message with lively energy and excitement. Their shouting broke through the silence of the night, and the star broke through the darkness.

The psalm calls us to "please stand up for the poor, help the children of the needy, come down hard on the cruel tyrants."

How do we stand up with lively energy for those who are oppressed so that change happens? How can you help the children of the needy with an excitement that gets something done? How do we speak into cruel systems with exuberant witness so lasting transformation occurs?

Where do we need to break through the darkness, silence, or the noise of injustice that is occurring around us?

Prayer

God of light and justice, fill our voices with the joy of Your coming and the boldness of Your truth that we might break through the noise with love, stand up for the hurting with hope, and shout with exuberance the good news of Your transforming grace. Amen.

Question

Where in your life or community do you feel called to raise your voice with "exuberant witness"—not in anger, but in love, justice, and hope—and what might that look like during this Advent season?

Second Wednesday of Advent

I Wonder, Do I Have the Courage of John the Baptist?

By Bishop Bob Farr

Scripture: Matthew 3:4-6 and Romans 15:3-6

> *John dressed in a camel-hair habit tied at the waist by a leather strap. He lived on a diet of locusts and wild field honey. People poured out of Jerusalem, Judea, and the Jordanian countryside to hear and see him in action. There at the Jordan River those who came to confess their sins were baptized into a changed life.*
>
> **Matthew 3:4-6 (MSG)**

> *That's exactly what Jesus did. He didn't make it easy for himself by avoiding people's troubles, but waded right in and helped out. "I took on the troubles of the troubled," is the way Scripture puts it. Even if it was written in Scripture long ago, you can be sure it's written for us. God wants the combination of his steady, constant calling and warm, personal counsel in Scripture to come to characterize us, keeping us alert for whatever he will do next. May our dependably steady and warmly personal God develop maturity in you so that you get along with each other as well as Jesus gets along with us all. Then we'll be a choir not our voices only, but our very lives singing in harmony in a stunning anthem to the God and Father of our Master Jesus!*
>
> **Romans 15:3-6 (MSG)**

Reflections

I wonder, do I have the courage of John the Baptist? John saw a broken world in need of a Messiah and knew his role required courage to prepare the way. He did not hesitate to speak about the trouble he witnessed. In the book of Romans, Paul reminds us that Jesus did the same thing. Jesus did not avoid people's troubles.

We can all look around and see people with troubles. We all encounter people with difficulties. As we desire to follow Jesus, we are called to take on the troubles of others. I know I don't always make that choice. I can come up with lots of excuses not to take on the trials of others. It takes courage to step into another's trouble. When talking about healthy boundaries, I often use the phrase, "Don't take on other people's monkeys." Yet, Jesus did.

God sent his son to take on the world's problems. Jesus came as a baby to grow into the man who "waded right in and helped out."

How many people around us struggle with grief and difficulties? They struggle to experience the joy that is so often promoted during the Advent season.

The scripture for today tells us that God wants us to have courage enough to wade into the trouble, having the characteristics of counsel and warmth, staying alert for what the Spirit will do next. Each time we take on the courage to wade in, God is developing maturity in us. We are reminded that we do not wade in by ourselves; the Spirit is working in and through us with each step.

Prayer

God of mercy and strength, give us the courage of John and the compassion of Jesus so we do not turn away from the troubles of others. Instead, with the guidance of Your Spirit, help us wade in with hope, healing, and love. Amen.

Questions

Who do you know who needs to hear about the gift of Jesus, the one who "took on the troubles of the troubled"?

Where do we need to wade into trouble?

Second Thursday of Advent

I Wonder, Do I Show Grace?

Bishop Bob Farr

Scripture: Isaiah 11:6-9

A Living Knowledge of God

The wolf will romp with the lamb,
the leopard sleep with the kid.
Calf and lion will eat from the same trough,
and a little child will tend them.
Cow and bear will graze the same pasture,
their calves and cubs grow up together,
and the lion eat straw like the ox.
The nursing child will crawl over rattlesnake dens,
the toddler stick his hand down the hole of a serpent.
Neither animal nor human will hurt or kill
on my holy mountain.
The whole earth will be brimming with knowing
God-Alive,
a living knowledge of God ocean-deep, ocean-wide.

Isaiah 11:6-9 (MSG)

Reflections

I wonder, do I show grace?

Yesterday, we read about having the courage of John the Baptist. John is often remembered as pushy—not what someone would call "grace-filled." However, grace comes to John the Baptist, to me, and to you through the Holy Spirit. We are all grace-filled.

When I read the verses from Isaiah, I can't imagine a cow and a bear in the same pasture or a nursing child crawling over a rattlesnake den. It sounds unbelievable to me. I grew up in the country. These images don't make sense to me.

However, these images display the wonder of a great reversal where God's presence and peace transform the world. They remind me that God's grace can take seemingly opposite things and use them for a purpose. God takes each of us and all that we are (good and bad), and through grace, God can put us into action to make the world a better place.

Considering this scripture, maybe one purpose of this season is to see the earth brimming with God. Once again, jumping ahead in the story, we are told after Jesus' birth, Mary spent time pondering. I think she was pondering the whole earth brimming with knowing God-Alive, a living knowledge of God ocean-deep, ocean-wide.

God's grace comes into our broken world, dwelling with us to show us that the earth can and does brim with knowing God-Alive—that moment when we think this is the way it is supposed to be. If we could just bottle that feeling. But it doesn't work that way. Those incredible moments are a blessing, but so are the messy ones—even when we can't imagine it or it just seems crazy. God's grace shows up in all of those places. That's how grace works.

How can we acknowledge, express, and share grace

this season so that others can see a vision of the world transformed by God's presence and peace?

Prayer

Gracious God, in the beauty and in the mess, in what makes sense and what seems impossible, help us to see Your presence brimming in the world and fill us with Your grace so that we may share it freely and help reveal Your peace to others. Amen.

Question

How can we acknowledge, express, and share grace this season so that others can see a vision of the world transformed by God's presence and peace?

Second Friday of Advent

I Wonder, Who are the Insiders of God's Love?

By Bishop Bob Farr

Scripture: Romans 15:7-13

> *So reach out and welcome one another to God's glory. Jesus did it; now you do it! Jesus, staying true to God's purposes, reached out in a special way to the Jewish insiders so that the old ancestral promises would come true for them. As a result, the non-Jewish outsiders have been able to experience mercy and to show appreciation to God. Just think of all the Scriptures that will come true in what we do! For instance:*
>
> *Then I'll join outsiders in a hymn-sing;*
> *I'll sing to your name!*
>
> *And this one:*
>
> *Outsiders and insiders, rejoice together!*
>
> *And again:*
>
> *People of all nations, celebrate God!*
> *All colors and races, give hearty praise!*
>
> *And Isaiah's word:*
>
> *There's the root of our ancestor Jesse,*
> *breaking through the earth and growing tree tall,*
> *Tall enough for everyone everywhere to see and take hope!*
>
> *Oh! May the God of green hope fill you up with joy, fill you up with peace, so that your believing lives, filled with the life-giving energy of the Holy Spirit, will brim over with hope!*

Romans 15:7-13 (MSG)

Reflections

All week, we have been reading about John the Baptist as the one who came to prepare the way for Jesus. John's lineage instituted him as an insider, while his ministry to prepare the way for Jesus made him an outsider.

We struggle with the distinction between insiders and outsiders in the church, in the country, and in the world. Paul, the writer of Romans, also struggled with understanding who was an insider and who was an outsider. Early in his "ministry career," he was an influential oppressor of the movement of Jesus' followers. He considered himself an insider with the mission to eliminate the outsiders. Then he had an encounter with Jesus, and he found himself an outsider.

The scripture for today declares we will gather with those who are considered outsiders and sing God's praises. We will all join the outsiders in a hymn sing. Can you imagine what our church music directors would think if the whole choir was made up of those outside the church, the Christmas cantata being sung by those who didn't attend choir practice the prior Wednesday?

This is another example of scripture's great reversal. We think it is one way, but it is not. We want to draw lines between those who are inside God's love and those who are outside. In this case, it was the Jews who were the insiders and the Gentiles who were considered outsiders. The people who thought they had a relationship with God and those who did not. Jesus erased that line. Maybe you need to be reminded that the life-giving hope of Jesus Christ is yours. You are on the inside of God's love, even if you didn't make it to choir practice.

Who do you know feels like or has been told they are an outsider or excluded from the love of Jesus Christ? How can you reach out to those people? How can we discuss and bridge the line between insider and outsider, blending the two into one family of God? One, but many; many, but one. Individuality and unity, all in one. Jesus makes it possible.

Prayer

God of insiders and outsiders, break down the barriers we build. Remind us that Your love knows no bounds, and help us sing with joy alongside all Your children—one family united in the hope of Jesus Christ. Amen.

Question

How does the idea that God includes both insiders and outsiders challenge or encourage you, and what might it mean for how we welcome others during this Advent season?

Second Saturday of Advent

I Still Wonder

By Bishop Bob Farr

Scripture: Romans 15:13

> *Oh! May the God of green hope fill you up with joy, fill you up with peace, so that your believing lives, filled with the life-giving energy of the Holy Spirit, will brim over with hope!*

Romans 15:13 (MSG)

Reflections

I still wonder ...

Can I see the star again? Can I smell the animals in the stable? Can I visualize the kings delivering their gifts? Can I hear the angels sing? Can I find the courage to shout out, "Messiah, Savior, King, Friend, Jesus"?

As I ponder these questions, I am reminded of all the nativity scenes that are displayed in our home during the Advent and Christmas seasons. Susan and I have collected many different types over the years, each one different and beautiful in its own way. Like the different nativity reenactments that take place in our churches, they allow us to catch a glimpse into the night that brought to us the Baby Jesus, the one who would erase the lines between insiders and outsiders. Through the imagination these manger scenes evoke in me, I can almost see the beauty of the star that night, smell the earthy tones of the animals in the stable, hear the pure tones and melodies of the angels singing, and feel the awe of the kings as they deliver their gifts.

As you peer into this season, may you also catch a glimpse of the star, the animals, the angels, and the kings. May you find your courage to wade right in with counsel and warmth to help prepare the road for others who are seeking light and joy, maybe through a fog of doubt, loneliness, or trouble. May we shout, "Messiah, Savior, King, Friend, Jesus," and provide an exuberant witness to the grace and inclusiveness of a God who desperately loves us all. May we all experience something deeper this season: awe, wonder, hope.

Prayer

Dear God, through Jesus Christ, invade our spirits and reawaken our wonder and curiosity. In the divine, sometimes we are like a person lost at night, unable to see the faint flickers of Jesus' light. Help us see the light of Jesus Christ. Help us invite you more and more into our lives. Give us the patience to wait, expect, and see the light of Christ. Fill us with hope, love, joy, and peace in this season of Advent. Help us once again catch the wonder of God through Jesus. Amen.

Question

What part of the nativity story speaks most deeply to you this year, and how might it inspire you to share Christ's light and love with someone who feels outside the story?

GROUP STUDY GUIDE

Second Week of Advent

The Wonder of Preparation

In week two of Advent, Bishop Bob Farr invites us to rediscover "wonder" as a spiritual posture. Through the example of John the Baptist, we are reminded that preparing the way for Christ calls for courage, grace, and a vision that sees beneath the surface. From ancient prophets to modern-day disciples, we are called to build straight paths, proclaim justice with joy, and embrace the mystery of God's coming presence with awe.

Welcome and Opening Prayer (5 minutes)

Invite a group member to open with one of the provided daily prayers or a prayer of their own.

Scripture Reading (10 minutes)

Read aloud one or more of the week's key scriptures:

Matthew 3:1–6

Isaiah 11:1–10

Psalm 72:1–7

Romans 15:3–13

Discussion Questions (30-35 minutes)

Use the questions below to foster conversation. Encourage honest sharing and mutual support.

Preparation (Matthew 3:1–12; Isaiah 11:1–10)

What does it mean for you to prepare the way for Christ today?

How can we cultivate spiritual "wonder" in a world full of noise and distraction?

Spiritual Construction (Isaiah 11:1–5)

What spiritual "roadwork" might God be calling you to this season?

How can patience play a role in preparing the way?

Exuberant Witness (Psalm 72:1–7)

What would it look like for your voice to be filled with "exuberant witness"?

How can joy and justice go hand-in-hand in our message?

Courageous Compassion (Matthew 3:4–6; Romans 15:3–6)

Where are you being called to wade into someone else's trouble with courage?

What does it mean to reflect Jesus' steady and personal care?

Grace in the Reversal (Isaiah 11:6–9)

How do you experience God's grace in both beautiful and messy moments?

What's one way you can show grace this week?

One Family in Hope (Romans 15:7–13)

Who are the "outsiders" in your community, and how can you welcome them?

How does it feel to know that God's hope is for everyone?

Living in the Light (Romans 15:13; Luke 2:19)

What part of the nativity story speaks most deeply to you this year?

How can you share that wonder and light with someone who feels left out?

Closing Time (5 minutes)

Prayer: Close with one of the daily prayers or invite a member to offer a prayer.

Challenge: This week, live out the wonder of Advent by intentionally preparing the way for someone else. Choose one person—perhaps a neighbor, co-worker, or someone who feels like an "outsider"—and do something small but meaningful to reflect Christ's light to them. It could be:

- A handwritten note of encouragement
- An invitation to a holiday service or event
- A simple act of kindness done with joy and intentionality

How did this act help prepare a road for Christ's love to travel into someone else's life—and into yours?

Third Week

of Advent

Bishop Sharma D. Lewis Logan

Third Sunday of Advent

Praise the Lord!

By Bishop Sharma D. Lewis Logan

Scripture: Psalm 146:5-10

> *Blessed are those who help is the God of Jacob, whose hope is in the Lord their God. He is the Maker of heaven and earth, the sea, and everything in them—he remains faithful forever. He upholds the cause of the oppressed and gives food to the hungry. The Lord sets prisoners free, the Lord gives sight to the blind, the Lord lifts up those who are bowed down, the Lord loves the righteous. The Lord watches over the foreigner and sustains the fatherless and the widow, but he frustrates the ways of the wicked. The Lord reigns forever, your God, O Zion, for all generations. Praise the Lord.*

Psalm 146:5-10 (NIV)

Reflections

As a child growing up in Statesboro, Georgia, our weekly Christian ritual was attending Brannen Chapel United Methodist Church. On Saturday evenings, we would complete our Sunday School lessons and lay out our clothes for the next morning. Every Sunday morning, we would hear my mother's favorite song, "May the Work I've Done Speak for Me," play on the record player. My father would smoke his pipe, which would always compete with the aroma of breakfast. He would sit in his favorite chair by the window, allowing the sunlight to shine in as he caught up on his weekly readings from the *Statesboro Herald*.

I remember every Sunday sitting in the front pew with my father and listening to our pastor's message. One of my fondest memories of our church was the changing of the paraments on the altar. My mother's responsibility as head usher was to keep up with this yearly assignment. It was not until I became older that I understood the liturgical colors or their meanings.

The Advent season was an active time in the life of Brannen Chapel. It would bring families together to read the Advent devotions and light the Advent wreath. It would allow us, as families, to decorate the church with poinsettias and evergreens and set up the Chrismon tree in the narthex. It would allow the mothers of the church to prepare their favorite Christmas dishes, and it would enable our church choirs to sing carols for the community and church programs.

As we examine our text, the psalmist is encouraging us to trust in the Lord for who God is and for what God does. Psalm 146 is the first of the five psalms known as the "Hallelujah Psalms." According to The New Interpreter's Dictionary of the Bible, "Praise is defined as the human activity, oriented toward others in a gesture of gratitude and exaltation for the person, accomplishments, and presence of others." In this text, the psalmist describes the Lord as the creator, a faithful and compassionate healer, and a liberator who reigns forever.

As we enter the third week of Advent, let our overflowing joy and praise of Jesus Christ permeate our hearts. In this busy season, let us not forget to praise our long-awaited Savior, who came into this sinful world to give us hope. As the psalmist reminds us in Psalm 100:4, "Enter into his gates with thanksgiving and his courts with praise; give thanks to him and praise his name."

Prayer

Praise the Lord for his goodness and grace! Amen.

Question

How do you give God praise during this Advent season?

Third Monday of Advent

Miracles!

By Bishop Sharma D. Lewis Logan

Scripture: Acts 5:12-16

> *The apostles performed many signs and wonders among the people. And all the believers used to meet together in Solomon's Colonnade. No one else dared join them, even though they were highly regarded by the people. Nevertheless, more and more men and women believed in the Lord and were added to their number. As a result, people brought the sick into the streets and laid them on beds and mats so that at least Peter's shadow might fall on some of them as he passed by. Crowds gathered also from the town around Jerusalem, bringing their sick and those tormented by impure spirits, and all of them were healed.*
>
> **Acts 5:12-16 (NIV)**

Reflections

Do you believe that signs, wonders, and miracles still exist in 2025? Or do you believe in coincidence or luck? Albert Einstein stated, "There are only two ways to live your life. One is as if nothing is a miracle. The other is as if everything is a miracle."

According to The New Interpreter's Dictionary of the Bible, a "miracle functions as a sign, a communication of

God's relationship with humankind and history." The Nelson Bible Dictionary describes a miracle as "a historical event or natural phenomena that appears to violate natural laws."

In our passage for today's reading, we witness the apostles performing many miracles among the people in Jerusalem. It is noted in the text that many Jewish people were being healed from all types of diseases, including those demon-possessed.

In the text, more and more people were joining the faith, and as a result, the popularity of the apostles was increasing. During this time, it was encouraged to bring the sick and afflicted and lay them in the streets so that the miracle of Peter's shadow would heal them from their diseases. In addition to these miracles, the reader learns that many people from surrounding communities were coming to be healed.

As we prepare for this Advent season, I believe the greatest miracle was the birth of our Lord and Savior, born to a virgin who was faithful, favored, and ultimately fulfilled God's promise.

I have always been in awe as I hear the miracles that are simply unexplained; for example, near-fatal car accidents, the birth of a child in a car, or a plane that erupts in flames landing in Tokyo with all surviving passengers. I personally believe that miracles are happening all around us, but we have ceased to believe in God's supernatural abilities.

As I revisit my own medical journey in 2018 and 2019, I'm a living witness to the miracle of intercessory prayer and spiritual healing. I was diagnosed with avascular necrosis (AVN) in the fall of 2018. The primary treatment for AVN is a total hip replacement. Unfortunately, my diagnosis led to four left hip surgeries, two infections, several blood and iron transfusions, x-rays, scans, and many hours of inpatient and outpatient therapy.

So, when people ask me if I still believe in miracles, my urgent response is yes—you're looking at one! Me!

Prayer

Lord, protect us as miracles are happening all around us. Amen.

Question

Have you experienced a miracle in your life? Please reflect on the goodness of God's grace.

Third Tuesday of Advent

The Christmas Blues

By Bishop Sharma D. Lewis Logan

Scripture: Psalm 42:5

> *Why, my soul, are you downcast? Why so disturbed within me? Put your hope in God, for I will yet praise him, my Savior and God.*
>
> **Psalm 42:5 (NIV)**

Reflections

Have you ever experienced what psychologists call the "Christmas Blues?" Christmas Blues is characterized by the depressive state that many individuals experience during the Christmas season. The Christmas season, filled with family gatherings, late-night shopping, wrapping gifts, and church events, is overshadowed by feelings of anxiety, sadness, frustration, and a state of loneliness for some individuals.

According to psychologists, Christmas Blues can occur for several reasons, contributing to a sense of sadness, loss, uncertainty, and depression during the holiday season.

On December 12, 2020, I experienced my own Christmas Blues when my mother transitioned into the arms of God after declining from a freak accident that left her with several vertebrae broken in her back. As a family, we tried to cover our pain and sorrow with the virtue of hope, hoping that the report from the doctor's "failure to thrive" was a misdiagnosis.

My mother endured the pain by listening to the Word of God and to her favorite gospel Christmas songs. My siblings clung to the hope that she would recover, but listening to the hospice nurse describe the reality of the situation prompted me to slip into my own Christmas Blues.

I remember picking up The Upper Room to discover the verse for the day: "Why, my soul, are you downcast? Why so disturbed within me? Put your hope in God, for I will yet praise him, my Savior and my God."

Why, my soul, are you downcast? Wasn't it obvious that my ninety-year-old matriarch was slowly slipping away in front of our faces? As I continued to read, I glanced over the verse that states, "Put your hope in God, for I will yet praise him, my Savior and God." As a trained pastor, I couldn't help but notice that verse five was repeated again in verse eleven.

"Hope," as described in The New Interpreter's Dictionary of the Bible, is looking forward with confidence to a future good. We hoped that things would get back to normal. We hoped that my mother would experience a miraculous healing on this side of glory.

However, during her transition, God showed me that my mother knew in her last days that her hope was in Jesus

Christ. As the psalmist David writes in Psalm 130:5, "I wait for the Lord, my whole being waits, and in his word, I put my hope."

Prayer

Lord, my hope is in the Lord who made heaven and earth. Amen.

Question

How do you handle the Christmas Blues?

Third Wednesday of Advent

The Simple Touch

By Bishop Sharma D. Lewis Logan

Scripture: Matthew 8:14-17, 28-34

> *When Jesus came into Peter's house, he saw Peter's mother-in-law lying in bed with a fever. He touched her hand and the fever left her, and she got up and began to wait on him.*
>
> *When evening came, many who were demon-possessed were brought to him, and he drove out the spirits with a word and healed all the sick. This was to fulfill what was spoken through the prophet Isaiah:*
>
> *"He took up our infirmities and bore our diseases."*
>
> **Matthew 8:14-17 (NIV)**

> *When he arrived at the other side in the region of the Gadarenes, two demon-possessed men coming from the tombs met him. They were so violent that no one could pass that way. "What do you want with us, Son of God?" they shouted. Have you come here to torture us before the appointed time?" Some distance from them a large herd of pigs was feeding. The demons begged Jesus, "If you drive us out, send us into the herd of pigs." He said to them, "Go!" So, they came out and went into the pigs, and the whole herd rushed down the steep bank in the lake and died in the water. Those tending the pigs ran off, went*

into the town and reported all this, including what had happened to the demon-possessed men. Then the whole town went out to meet Jesus. And when they saw him, they pleaded with him to leave their region.

Matthew 8:28-34 (NIV)

Something happened, and now I know, he touched me and made me whole.

Bill Gaither, 1963
He Touched Me

Reflections

When examining the pericopes for today, we see two distinct healing stories. Peter's mother-in-law, an unnamed woman, is miraculously healed by a simple touch from Jesus, followed by two demon-possessed men whose simple response to "Go" caused the demons to flee into a herd of pigs, bringing them to their sudden death.

The text reveals that Peter's mother-in-law was immediately healed, and as a result, she showed her gratitude by serving Jesus and his disciples. The reader is never told how long Peter's mother-in-law and the demon-possessed men waited and anticipated their healing. However, in both accounts, we witness Jesus' capacity to love everyone regardless of their name or social status. Jesus loved this unnamed woman, which serves to remind us that he loves each and every one of us, no matter if we are a sinner or a saint. In Jesus' eyes, we are the same and of equal importance and value. Throughout his ministry, Jesus demonstrates his love for the least and lost, interacting with the poor, the sick, the hungry, the imprisoned, and the demon-possessed.

Matthew 8:28-34 is another example of the love that Jesus demonstrated to the sick by healing the two demon-possessed men in the region of the Gadarenes, mainly inhabited by the Gentiles. According to Jewish law, the two demon-possessed men were unclean because they were Gentiles, demon-possessed, and they lived in the cemetery. Despite the Jewish culture, Jesus, through his healing actions, continued to demonstrate the value of human life. Similarly to the woman with the issue of blood, both stories highlight the love of Jesus, the healing touch, and the fulfilled prophecy of Isaiah 53:4-5: "Surely he took up our pain and bore our suffering … and by his wounds we are healed."

As we approach this Advent season, what lives are we touching within our church, our community, and our world?

Prayer

Lord, please allow us to touch the poor, the sick, the hungry, and the demon-possessed. Amen.

Question

What are the lessons we learn from the healing of Peter's mother-in-law and the two demon-possessed men?

Third Thursday of Advent

We Are One

By Bishop Sharma D. Lewis Logan

Scripture: Galatians 3:23-29

> *Before the coming of this faith, we were held in custody under the law, locked up until the faith that was to come would be revealed. So, the law was our guardian until Christ came that we might be justified by faith. Now that this faith has come, we are no longer under a guardian. So, in Christ Jesus you are all children of God through faith, for all of you who were baptized into Christ have clothed yourselves with Christ. There is neither Jew nor Gentile, neither slave nor free, nor is there male and female, for you all are one in Christ Jesus. If you belong to Christ, then you are Abraham's seed and heirs according to the promise.*

Galatians 3:23-29 (NIV)

Reflections

Growing up in Statesboro, Georgia, I always enjoyed attending Vacation Bible School at our home church, Brannen Chapel United Methodist Church. My favorite Vacation Bible School experience was always making new friends and rekindling old friendships. We would paint, play, go on a variety of field trips, and we would always have "musical moments."

These musical moments included learning new dances, playing new instruments, or learning new songs. At the end of Vacation Bible School, each class was responsible for sharing what they had learned during the week.

I will never forget the theme: "We Are One," accompanied by the theme song, "They'll Know We are Christians by Our Love."

> *And they'll know we are Christians by our love, by our love. Yeah, they'll know we are Christians by our love.*
>
> **Peter Scholtes 1969**
> *They Will Know We are Christians by Our Love*

This song, written in the 1960s by Father Peter Scholtes, a Catholic priest, has been recorded by a variety of Christian artists and featured in the opening of the Christian movie *A Distant Thunder,* part of the *A Thief in the Night* series.

As a result of our theme, we were taught the importance of understanding diversity, whether racially or culturally. Our group decided to demonstrate our musical talents by learning the elements of sign language to "They'll Know We are Christians by Our Love." To say the least, this was a hit for our presentation!

As we examine our passage for today, the Apostle Paul emphasizes the unity found in Christ, where differences between Jew and Gentile, slave and free, and male and female were not important because, as Paul reminds us, we are one in Christ and heirs to Abraham's promises found in Genesis 12:3 and 15:6.

Living in Mississippi, I notice that there is still a great divide between ethnicity, gender, and socioeconomic status. It is still being played out in education, politics, and the church. Unfortunately, our clean water crisis in 2023 proved this distinction. However, the greatest nugget in this text is the Apostle Paul's explanation that the arrival of Jesus Christ frees us from being under the law because we are joint heirs to the kingdom of God (Romans 8:17).

Prayer

O Lord, let us recognize that we are One in Jesus Christ. Amen.

Question

There are still divisions in our society. How do we become one with Christ and one with each other?

Third Friday of Advent

Identity

By Bishop Sharma D. Lewis Logan

Scripture: Galatians 4:1-7

> *What I am saying is that as long as an heir is underage, he is no different from a slave, although he owns the whole estate.*
>
> *The heir is subject to guardians and trustees until the time set by his father. So also, when we were underage, we were in slavery under the elemental spiritual forces of the world.*
>
> *But when the set time had fully come, God sent his Son, born of a woman, born under the law, to redeem those under the law, that we might receive adoption to sonship.*
>
> *Because you are his sons, God sent the Spirit of his Son into our hearts, the Spirit who calls out, "Abba, Father." So you are no longer a slave, but God's child; and since you are his child, God has made you also an heir.*
>
> **Galatians 4:1-7 (NIV)**

Reflections

I remember when Joyce, a single woman, wanted desperately to have children but decided, after several failed relationships, to adopt a child. She decided that she was too old to have children, and the thought of marriage was nowhere on the horizon. She researched the matter, attended classes, discussed it with her family, and began preparing for a legal adoption.

One day, she called me, her voice filled with excitement, to tell me she had finally been approved by the adoption agency. My schedule didn't permit me to join the family at the courthouse, but the Facebook pictures captured the joy and excitement in the courtroom. Finally, she brought home Autumn, a five-year-old little girl who was very inquisitive and wanted to be loved.

In Galatians 4:1-7, Paul writes that in Christ, we have a new identity, adoption, and inheritance in the kingdom of God. First, our identity is depicted as a slave. "When we were underage, we were in slavery under the elemental spiritual forces of the world (v. 3). Secondly, through faith in Jesus Christ, we are adopted as God's children. Paul says, "But when the set time had fully come, God sent his Son, born of a woman, born under the law, to redeem those under the law, that we might receive adoption to sonship. (vv. 4-5).

Finally, we are heirs to the eternal reward. John 3:16 reminds us, "For God so loved the world that he gave his one and only Son, that whoever believes in him shall not perish but have eternal life."

Galatians 4:1-7 emphasizes the power of Christ's arrival, positions us as believers to receive salvation, and grants us the status of heirs to the kingdom.

This Advent season, as we reflect on Christ's coming, we are reminded that our truest identity is not rooted in our past, our status, or even our earthly families—but in the love of a God who has chosen to adopt us as beloved children. Just as Autumn's adoption marked a turning point in her life, our adoption through Christ marks a powerful spiritual transformation. We are no longer defined by what was but by the promise of what is and what will be.

Let this be a season when we reclaim our identity as heirs of God—living not in fear or striving but in gratitude and hope. As we prepare for Christmas, may we embrace the truth that we are wanted, known, and deeply loved by our Heavenly Father. And may we extend that same spirit of adoption to others: welcoming, including, and encouraging those who need to know they belong.

Prayer

Lord, let us know that our identity is in Jesus Christ, and we are adopted as children of God and heirs to the grace of God. Amen.

Question

When did you realize, as a believer, that you had a new identity in Jesus Christ?

Third Saturday of Advent

Suffering

By Bishop Sharma D. Lewis Logan

Scripture: Psalm 80:1-7, 17-19

Hear us, Shepherd of Israel,
you who lead Joseph like a flock.
You who sit enthroned between the cherubim, shine forth
before Ephraim, Benjamin and Manasseh.
Awaken your might; come and save us.
Restore us, O God; make your face shine on us,
that we may be saved.

How long, Lord God Almighty, will your anger smolder
against the prayers of your people?
You have fed them with the bread of tears;
you have made them drink tears by the bowlful.
You have made us an object of derision to our neighbors,
and our enemies mock us.

Restore us, God Almighty;
make your face shine on us,
that we may be saved.

Let your hand rest on the man at your right hand,
the son of man you have raised up for yourself.
Then we will not turn away from you;
revive us, and we will call on your name.
Restore us, Lord God Almighty;
make your face shine on us, that we may be saved.

Psalm 80:1-7, 17-19 (NIV)

Reflections

According to scholars, Psalm 80 is a communal lament and prayer for restoration. The psalmist communicates the suffering of the people of Israel and their desire for God's intervention. The psalmist expresses a deep concern for God's face to shine upon Israel—found in verses three, seven, and nineteen—therefore bringing salvation and relief from their sorrow.

According to The New Interpreter's Dictionary of the Bible, "Suffering means agony, affliction or distress; intense pain or sorrow." Suffering has been a part of the human experience since Adam and Eve fell in the Garden of Eden. Suffering has been a part of the black and brown culture for decades. In the African American culture, we suffered during slavery, we suffered during the civil rights era, and we've suffered to be noticed and not overlooked.

The Bible reveals that some suffering is the result of sin, and some scholars have depicted that suffering helps believers identify with Christ. According to Romans 5:3, "We also glory in our sufferings, because we know that suffering produces perseverance; perseverance, character; and character, hope.

Scholars reveal that suffering not only shapes our character but refines us as God's children. I believe that the purpose of suffering is not to destroy us but to purge and refine us.

As I walk this Christian journey, my suffering has strengthened my faith. First Peter 1:7 states "that the proven genuineness of your faith—of greater worth than gold, which perishes even though refined by fire—may result in praise, glory and honor when Jesus Christ is revealed."

Suffering causes us to depend on and trust God in all circumstances. The psalmist David states in Psalm 34:18, "The Lord is close to the brokenhearted and saves those who are crushed in spirit."

Psalm 80 is a powerful prayer that represents our faith, hope, and desire for God's intervention in the face of hardship and mockery from one's enemies. The psalm uses the vine as a metaphor to represent God's love for God's people and to illustrate the suffering of Israel and their desire for restoration.

The repeated theme of the psalm expresses the hope for grace and favor: "Restore us, Lord God Almighty; make your face shine on us, that we may be saved."

Prayer

"The Lord bless you and keep you; the Lord make his face shine on you and be gracious to you; the Lord turn his face toward you and give you peace" (Numbers 6:24-26, NIV).

Question

Reflect on how God has intervened in your suffering. How does God's intervening refine you as a child of God?

GROUP STUDY GUIDE

Third Week of Advent

Reflecting on the Nearness of God

This third week of Advent, Bishop Sharma D. Lewis Logan invites us to reflect on the nearness of God through themes of praise, miracles, grief, healing, unity, identity, and suffering. Through powerful personal testimony and deep scriptural engagement, we are reminded that Advent is a season of both joy and honest lament—a time when God's presence shows up in miraculous touches, communal pain, and the quiet hope that lives even in the shadows of sorrow.

Welcome and Opening Prayer (5 minutes)

Invite a group member to open with the provided daily prayer or one of their own.

Scripture Reading (5–10 minutes)

Read aloud one or more of the week's key scriptures:

Psalm 146:5–10

Acts 5:12–16

Psalm 42:5

Matthew 8:14–17, 28–34

Galatians 3:23–29

Galatians 4:1–7

Psalm 80:1–7, 17–19

Discussion Questions (30–35 minutes)

Use the questions below to foster conversation. Encourage honest sharing and mutual support.

Praise in the Midst (Psalm 146)

What does it mean to "Praise the Lord" in both good and hard times?

How can personal memories of faith shape our Advent practices today?

Miracles and Belief (Acts 5)

Do you believe in miracles today? How have you seen or experienced one?

How can we become more aware of the miraculous in ordinary life?

The Christmas Blues (Psalm 42)

How do you deal with sadness or grief during the holiday season?

How can the church provide space for both joy and lament during Advent?

Healing and Inclusion (Matthew 8)

What can we learn from Jesus' touch—both to the unnamed woman and the demon-possessed men?

Who are we called to "touch" with compassion in our communities?

Unity in Christ (Galatians 3)

What divisions still exist in our communities?

How can the church embody Paul's message that "we are one in Christ Jesus"?

Identity and Adoption (Galatians 4)

When did you first realize your identity as a child of God?

What does it mean to be an heir of God's promises?

Suffering and Restoration (Psalm 80)

How have you experienced God's presence during a time of suffering?

What does it mean for God's "face to shine upon us" today?

Closing Time (5 minutes)

Prayer: Choose one of the week's prayers or invite a group member to close in prayer.

Challenge: This week, identify someone who might be struggling with loneliness, grief, or illness—and find a way to be a gentle "touch of Christ" for them. Whether through a visit, a note, or a simple gesture of kindness, let your life echo the healing and unity described in this week's scriptures.

Fourth Week
of Advent

Bishop Debra Wallace-Padgett

Fourth Sunday of Advent

Gospel of God

By Bishop Debra Wallace-Padgett

Scripture: Romans 1:1-7

> *Paul, a servant of Christ Jesus, called to be an apostle, set apart for the gospel of God, which he promised beforehand through his prophets in the holy scriptures, the gospel concerning his Son, who was descended from David according to the flesh and was declared to be Son of God with power according to the spirit of holiness by resurrection from the dead, Jesus Christ our Lord, through whom we have received grace and apostleship to bring about the obedience of faith among all the gentiles for the sake of his name, including you who are called to belong to Jesus Christ,*
>
> *To all God's beloved in Rome, who are called to be saints:*
>
> *Grace to you and peace from God our Father and the Lord Jesus Christ.*
>
> **Romans 1:1-7 (NRSV)**

Reflections

When reading the book of Romans in the past, I never noticed the words "Gospel of God." Yet this time, the phrase jumped out at me as if it was italicized, in all caps, and in bold. Reading scripture is sometimes like that. No matter how often we have read a particular passage, God is ready to speak a fresh word to us through it. I am glad this happened to me with today's scripture passage because the concept it offers is central to Christian theology.

"Gospel" (*evangelion* in Greek) is typically used by Paul in Romans to reference Jesus, the second person of the Three in One God. "Gospel of God" is another way for Paul to say "The Good News of Jesus Christ." What better time for us to reflect upon the "Gospel of God" than a few short days prior to the celebration of the birth of Jesus!

N.T. Wright reminds us that Paul, the author of Romans, is both a Jewish and Roman citizen. His Jewish heritage enables him to connect the Gospel of God with the prophecies of Isaiah 40 and 52 about a messenger bringing the good news of victory to Jerusalem, resulting in the restoration of Judah. On the other hand, as a citizen of Rome, Paul knows that evangelion is often a proclamation about a rising ruler (The New Interpreter's Bible, Romans, 415).

Paul boldly proclaims in today's passage that Jesus Christ fulfills Isaiah 40, 52, and more. Previously, God had sent judges, prophets, prophetesses, and kings to offer the Good News of forgiveness and new life. But humanity was unable to fully comprehend this message. So, God's Son, Jesus, entered the world through a young woman named Mary to communicate the Good News more clearly.

Jesus, God Incarnate, is the Gospel of God, the best news the world has ever experienced. Jesus is God's answer to the brokenness of the world.

Ask the struggling young man who has found hope

for the future in his newfound relationship with Jesus. Or the hungry child who is receiving nourishing meals while simultaneously learning the stories of Jesus from the nearby church that offers an after-school program. Or the mother who discovers peace and new life as she encounters Jesus through her Bible study. Or fill in the blank with situations where you know people have been changed by the Gospel of God.

By its very definition, the Gospel of God is meant to be shared. Accounts of this happening are described again and again in the first four books of the New Testament. The angel Gabriel does so with Mary (Luke 1:26-38), and then later, an unnamed angel comes to her husband, Joseph (Matthew 1:20-21). A heavenly host sings the Good News to the shepherds after being told by an angel of Jesus' birth (Luke 2:8-20). The elderly Prophet Simeon takes the eight-day-old Jesus in his arms in the temple, blesses God, and prophesizes about Jesus' future to Mary and Joseph (Luke 2:25-34). Soon thereafter, the 84-year-old prophetess comes on the scene while Simeon is holding Jesus. She offers prayers and talks about Jesus not only to his parents but also to other receptive listeners in the temple (Luke 2:36-38). Then, when Jesus is a young child, the Wise Men follow a star to Bethlehem to see Jesus (Matthew 2:1-12). Most significantly, Jesus proclaims the Gospel of God in word and deed throughout his ministry. And various people like the Samaritan woman (John 4:1-42) witness to all who will listen of Jesus' transforming power.

The phrase "Gospel of God" had not registered with

me in previous readings of Romans. How appropriate that it did so as I prepared this devotional for the season of the Christian year called Advent, when we anticipate the Good News of God coming from heaven to earth in the person of Jesus. May each of us experience and share this Good News in new ways today and every day.

Prayer

God, thank you for offering your Gospel to the world in the person of Jesus. Help me to experience and share Jesus in new ways this day. In the name of the Christ Child, I pray. Amen.

Questions

How is the "Gospel of God" in the person of Jesus changing you?

How and with whom will you share the Gospel of God today?

Fourth Monday of Advent

Singing a New Song

By Bishop Debra Wallace-Padgett

Scripture: Psalm 96

O sing to the Lord a new song;
sing to the Lord, all the earth.
Sing to the Lord; bless his name;
tell of his salvation from day to day.
Declare his glory among the nations,
his marvelous works among all the peoples.
For great is the Lord and greatly to be praised;
he is to be revered above all gods.
For all the gods of the peoples are idols,
but the Lord made the heavens.
Honor and majesty are before him;
strength and beauty are in his sanctuary.

Ascribe to the Lord, O families of the peoples,
ascribe to the Lord glory and strength.
Ascribe to the Lord the glory due his name;
bring an offering, and come into his courts.
Worship the Lord in holy splendor;
tremble before him, all the earth.

Say among the nations, "The Lord is king!
The world is firmly established; it shall never be moved.
He will judge the peoples with equity."
Let the heavens be glad, and let the earth rejoice;
let the sea roar and all that fills it;
let the field exult and everything in it.

Then shall all the trees of the forest sing for joy
before the Lord, for he is coming, or he is coming to judge the earth.
He will judge the world with righteousness
and the peoples with his truth.

Psalm 96 (NRSV)

Reflections

Christmas is around the corner! The day we have been anticipating for weeks is almost here!

The Christian new year launched four Sundays ago when we began Advent, our annual season of watching, waiting, and preparing for the coming of the Christ Child. As Advent draws to a close, we anticipate a truth proclaimed throughout the Bible and emphasized in one of this week's lectionary readings from the book of Psalms. In essence, the psalmist says, "God reigns."

God reigns, but we humans enjoy being in charge. I was reminded of this when my husband and my then eighteen-month-old granddaughter, Raylee, pulled a blade of grass from the ground and stood waving it at a flock of birds. When they didn't respond by flying down and eating it, she called in a demanding voice, "Birds! Birds!"

Though Raylee and humanity in general like to be in charge, this is not the way life works—and that is good because we do not always know what is best.

In addition, due to our human propensity to make wrong and self-centered choices, brokenness and pain continue to exist in this world. Even so, when it is all said and done, our God is in charge and ultimately reigns victoriously.

How do we respond to God's reign? The psalmist calls us to "sing a new song." Many biblical scholars believe that Psalm 96 references the song sung before the Ark of the Covenant in 1 Chronicles 16. This most holy of relics contained the stone tablets on which the Ten Commandments were inscribed and also served as a visible reminder that God was with the people of Israel. The "new song" of Psalm 96 describes God's way (The Ten Commandments), tells of God's presence among us (the Ark of the Covenant), and defines what it means to be God-followers.

For Christians, the birth of Christ adds additional verses to the new song. A verse referring to God coming down from heaven to earth to live among us through Jesus Christ's birth. Another verse describing Jesus' teachings and way. A crescendo to the final verse of an invitation for forgiveness, salvation, and new life for all the world through Jesus' death and resurrection.

What better time is there to proclaim this new song than as Christmas Day quickly approaches? On this fourth Monday of Advent, let us join the psalmist in "singing to God a new song." A song of God's presence in our lives. A song describing God's way through Jesus Christ. A song of forgiveness and new life made possible through Jesus Christ. Let us sing God's new song today and every day!

Prayer

God, thank you for being present in our lives and world. Thank you for the new song you are teaching us through Jesus Christ. Thank you for the opportunity to sing a new song during this Advent season and every day of the year. In the name of the Christ Child, we pray. Amen.

Question

What are the words of the new song that have special meaning to you this Advent season?

Fourth Tuesday of Advent

Gifts Packaged in Difficult Wrappings

By Bishop Debra Wallace-Padgett

Scripture: Matthew 1:18-25

> *Now the birth of Jesus the Messiah took place in this way. When his mother, Mary had been engaged to Joseph, but before they lived together, she was found to be pregnant from the Holy Spirit. Her husband Joseph, being a righteous man and unwilling to expose her to public disgrace, planned to divorce her quietly. But just when he had resolved to do this, an angel of the Lord appeared to him in a dream and said, "Joseph, son of David, do not be afraid to take Mary as your wife, for the child conceived in her is from the Holy Spirit. She will bear a son, and you are to name him Jesus, for he will save his people from their sins." All this took place to fulfill what had been spoken by the Lord through the prophet:*
>
> *"Look, the virgin shall become pregnant and give birth to a son, and they shall name him Emmanuel," which means, "God is with us." When Joseph awoke from sleep, he did as the angel of the Lord commanded him; he took her as his wife but had no marital relations with her until she had given birth to a son, and he named him Jesus.*

Matthew 1:18-25 (NRSV)

Reflections

Several years ago, I was introduced to the principle that "surprises are bad." This maxim is accurate when applied to leadership. After all, leaders, staff, and organizations do not like to learn secondhand about unexpected changes in direction, policy, or major decisions.

However, there are some instances when surprises are good, like the time that Lee and our children surprised me with a birthday party attended by twenty-five or so of my extended family at a state park. Or a gift that surpasses all expectations of the recipient. Or a surprise visit from a loved one. The best surprise of all is an unexpected gift from God. Though some gifts from God are obvious blessings, others are hidden by the package of difficult circumstances of their wrappings.

This is what Joseph receives in today's scripture passage. Although the unexpected gift of Jesus is great, the circumstances in which Joseph learns about him are difficult. It begins with news of Mary's pregnancy. At first, he assumes that the pregnancy means Mary is involved with another man and resolves to end the engagement quietly.

He lets go of his plan to break the engagement when he learns through a visitation of one of God's angels in a dream that Mary has not betrayed him, but "the child conceived in her is from the Holy Spirit" (Matthew 1:20). She is carrying the Savior of the world (Matthew 1:21)! This gift, this child will be a blessing, not only to Joseph and Mary but to the entire human race. However, the news of her pregnancy does not seem like a blessing to Joseph at first.

Have you ever received an unexpected gift from God that came out of difficult circumstances? Maybe it was a different answer to a prayer than the one you anticipated. Or a redirection of a dream that you had carried in your heart for a long time. Perhaps it required you to recalibrate how you looked at or even lived your life. Maybe it resulted in many tears and a broken heart. Although it may not have seemed like a gift at first, in retrospect, you came to embrace it as an amazing, wondrous blessing.

Songwriter Laura Story's song "Blessings" speaks to her personal experience in finding gifts wrapped in the difficult circumstances of her husband Martin's health issues. The first line of the chorus describes it this way:

Cause what if your blessings come through raindrops.

The chorus continues by asking if healing comes through tears, if God's nearness is found in the night, and if trials are mercies in disguise.

Jesus is an incredible blessing to Joseph and Mary, but there are tears and trials that come with him. First, they must work through Joseph's initial distrust of Mary's story. Next, the gossip from the village women is surely rampant and pointed, hurting them both!

Then, when Jesus is only a few days old, the Prophet Simeon says to Mary, "This child is destined for the falling and the rising of many in Israel ... and a sword will pierce your own soul too" (Luke 2:34-35). In other words, there is pain in Mary's and Joseph's future.

Despite the challenges that accompany Jesus' entrance into their lives, Joseph and Mary quickly come to understand that he is the greatest gift they will ever receive—the most wonderful gift the world will ever know. He is an unexpected gift, for sure, both in the timing of his arrival and also in the way he redefines what it means to be the long-awaited Savior.

Joseph responds in exactly the right way to the gift of Jesus: accepting him fully and without reservation. "When Joseph awoke from sleep, he did as the angel of the Lord commanded him; he took her as his wife but had no marital relations with her until she had given birth to a son, and he named him Jesus" (Matthew 1:24-25, NRSVue).

The leadership principle of "surprises are bad" is accurate in many situations but not when applied to God's unexpected gifts. Gifts such as Jesus in the life of Joseph and Mary ... like those received by Laura and Martin in his health difficulties ... and the blessings from God that are wrapped in the challenges of our lives.

During this Advent and Christmas season, I invite you to join me in considering the poignant questions raised in Laura Story's song. We can be sure of this: We live in a broken world full of difficulties and pain. We also serve a God who often brings unexpected gifts out of challenging situations.

Prayer

God, you are full of surprises. Thank you for the occasions in my life when you have brought blessings out of difficulties. Give me eyes to see the gifts that, at first glance, look like hardships.

Questions

When have you experienced an unexpected gift from God that at first looked like pain and hardship?

Where might this be occurring in your life right now?

Christmas Eve

Treasuring and Pondering

By Bishop Debra Wallace-Padgett

Scripture: Luke 2:1-14, 15-20

In those days a decree went out from Caesar Augustus that all the world should be registered. This was the first registration and was taken while Quirinius was governor of Syria. All went to their own towns to be registered. Joseph also went from the town of Nazareth in Galilee to Judea, to the city of David called Bethlehem, because he was descended from the house and family of David. He went to be registered with Mary, to whom he was engaged and who was expecting a child. While they were there, the time came for her to deliver her child. And she gave birth to her firstborn son and wrapped him in bands of cloth and laid him in a manger, because there was no place in the guest room.

The Shepherds and the Angels

Now in that same region there were shepherds living in the fields, keeping watch over their flock by night. Then an angel of the Lord stood before them, and the glory of the Lord shone around them, and they were terrified. But the angel said to them, "Do not be afraid, for see, I am bringing you good news of great joy for all the people: to you is born this day in the city of David a Savior, who is the Messiah, the Lord. This will be a sign for you: you will find a child wrapped in bands of cloth and lying in a manger." And suddenly there was with the angel a multitude of the heavenly host, praising God and saying,

"Glory to God in the highest heaven, and on earth peace among those whom he favors!"

When the angels had left them and gone into heaven, the shepherds said to one another, "Let us go now to Bethlehem and see this thing that has taken place, which the Lord has made known to us." So they went with haste and found Mary and Joseph and the child lying in the manger. When they saw this, they made known what had been told them about this child, and all who heard it were amazed at what the shepherds told them, and Mary treasured all these words and pondered them in her heart. The shepherds returned, glorifying and praising God for all they had heard and seen, just as it had been told them.

Luke 2:1-14,15-20 (NRSVue)

Reflections

I'm one of "those" grandparents. When the opportunity arises, I pull out my phone and show pictures of my husband Lee's and my grandchildren to relatives, colleagues, and even people I have just met. Then I smile appreciatively at the polite "oohs," "aahs," and comments that follow.

Positive words about those we dearly love are like treasures. Whether spoken about a child, spouse, parent, or friend, such affirmations warm one's heart. Perhaps this is why, when preparing to write today's Christmas Eve devotional, my eyes were drawn to Luke 2:19, "and Mary treasured all these words and pondered them in her heart."

Today's scripture passage describes how Mary and Joseph did more than show pictures of their amazing newborn Jesus to the shepherds who came to see him in Bethlehem. They welcomed the shepherds into the space where the baby Jesus was lying in a manger. Luke 2:17-18 tells us that when the shepherds saw him, "They made known what had been told them about this child" by the angel who had appeared earlier in the field where they were watching their sheep, "and all who heard it were amazed at what the shepherds told them."

There were at least two audiences who heard the shepherds' description of the angel's revelation in the field. Both groups were "amazed" at the shepherds' message. First, there was the general public. This consisted of anyone who would listen, including family, other shepherds, travelers along the way, and people encountered in the marketplace. It was a timeless story, too, that the shepherds surely continued to tell throughout their lifetimes.

Then there were Joseph and Mary. The shepherds' words reinforced what Mary and Joseph already knew. The Christ Child was more than their beautiful baby boy. He was the Savior of the world, the long-awaited Messiah, the One who would rule victoriously, mercifully, and justly forever and ever! The Good News of Jesus shared by the shepherds was surely a source of strength and joy to Mary and Joseph, not only at his birth but throughout his life.

On this Christmas Eve, I invite you to join me in treasuring and pondering the angel's words spoken to the shepherds about Jesus. May we feel the same joy in pondering the angel's Good News found in Luke 2 and throughout the Gospels as we do when positive words are spoken about our children, grandchildren, friends, and colleagues.

Prayer

God, thank you for the gift of Jesus, who came from heaven to earth over two thousand years ago. Give me new insights as I treasure and ponder the affirming words spoken about him to the Bethlehem shepherds. In the Christ Child's name, I pray. Amen.

Questions

How are the words of the angel in Luke 2:11-12 a treasure in my life? How about the song of the heavenly host in Luke 2:14?

What is a step I will take this Christmas Eve to ponder these words in my heart?

Christmas Day

Celebrate

By Bishop Debra Wallace-Padgett

Scripture: John 1:1-14

> *In the beginning was the Word, and the Word was with God, and the Word was God. He was in the beginning with God. All things came into being through him, and without him not one thing came into being. What has come into being in him was life, and the life was the light of all people. The light shines in the darkness, and the darkness did not overtake it.*
>
> *There was a man sent from God whose name was John. He came as a witness to testify to the light, so that all might believe through him. He himself was not the light, but he came to testify to the light. The true light, which enlightens everyone, was coming into the world.*
>
> *He was in the world, and the world came into being through him, yet the world did not know him. He came to what was his own, and his own people did not accept him. But to all who received him, who believed in his name, he gave power to become children of God, who were born, not of blood or of the will of the flesh or of the will of man, but of God.*
>
> *And the Word became flesh and lived among us, and we have seen his glory, the glory as of a father's only son, full of grace and truth.*
>
> **John 1:1-14 (NRSVue)**

Reflections

What is your favorite season?

That is a difficult question for me to answer as I love aspects of each season. The wintry snow covering the ground serves as a reminder of the fresh starts that abound in the rhythms of the year. The budding trees, blooming flowers, and signs of new life make spring an extraordinary season. The slower pace of summer is renewing. The resumption of a "normal" schedule amid the changing colors of fall is uplifting.

For Christ-followers, time is also marked by the Christian seasons. Advent, Epiphany, Lent, Eastertide, Pentecost, and even the sometimes seemingly endless part of the liturgical year called Ordinary Time all bring their unique emphasis and gifts to worship and life in Christ.

Then there is Christmas! Today, December 25, we are entering the twelve-day Christmas season. The weeks of Advent waiting have come and gone. Christmas Day is here, ushering in a season of celebration.

Yes, Christmas is a time for celebrating! Celebration is the right response to the announcement in John's Gospel that the Word became flesh and lived among us. Celebration is the natural reaction to the Good News that God came from heaven to earth in the person of Jesus so that we can know forgiveness and experience new and eternal life. Celebration is the appropriate action to take when we experience Christ's arrival in our world.

Participating in worship services, attending parties, exchanging gifts, sending cards, caroling, watching favorite Christmas movies, attending special dinners, reaching out to the lonely, and gathering as families and friends for service projects are a few examples of celebratory actions. Celebration is a sign that we see Jesus and believe in his name (John 1:12). The point is not the specific action but the fact that we intentionally celebrate the best news this world has ever known: "The Word became flesh and lived among us" (John 1:14a).

I love all the seasons of the year. On this day, my favorite one is the Christmas season and the spirit of celebration it brings. Have a blessed and celebratory Christmas Day and season!

Prayer

God, thank you for every season of the year. Today, I particularly celebrate the Christmas season and all that it means. May every celebratory action I take on this day be in response to the great news that the Word became flesh and lived among us. In the name of the Christ Child, I pray. Amen.

Question

What action will you take today to celebrate the Christmas season?

GROUP STUDY GUIDE

Fourth Week of Advent

Gospel of God

This final week of Advent and the Christmas celebration center on experiencing the Gospel of God—the Good News of Jesus Christ. Bishop Debra Wallace-Padgett explores how this Gospel shows up in surprising ways, in sacred songs, and even in difficult circumstances. The reflections culminate in a joyful Christmas call to celebrate Christ's birth and the light he brings into the world.

Welcome and Opening Prayer (5 minutes)

Invite a group member to open with the provided daily prayer or one of their own.

Scripture Reading (5-10 minutes)

Read aloud one or more of the week's key scriptures:

Romans 1:1–7

Psalm 96

Matthew 1:18–25

Luke 2:1–20

John 1:1–14

Discussion Questions (30-35 minutes)

Use the questions below to foster conversation. Encourage honest sharing and mutual support.

The Gospel of God (Romans 1:1–7)

How does the idea of the "Gospel of God" become more real to you during the Advent season?

In what ways have you seen or experienced the Gospel at work in the lives of others?

Singing a New Song (Psalm 96)

What "new song" is God teaching you this year?

How does your faith change when you focus on praising rather than worrying?

Gifts in Difficult Wrappings (Matthew 1:18–25)

Have you received a gift from God that was disguised as hardship at first?

How do you learn to recognize God's presence in the midst of uncertainty or disappointment?

Treasuring and Pondering (Luke 2:1–20)

What words or truths about Jesus do you treasure this season?

How can we intentionally "ponder" the meaning of Christ's birth in today's noisy world?

Celebrate! (John 1:1–14)

How does celebration reflect your understanding of the incarnation?

What meaningful action can you take this week to honor the joy of Christmas?

Closing Time (5 minutes)

Prayer: Choose one of the week's prayers or invite a group member to close in prayer.

Challenge: Encourage each participant to share the Gospel of God with one person this week—through words, acts of kindness, or simple presence.

Made in United States
Troutdale, OR
12/09/2025

43363852R00070